Teen

The ELI Readers collection is a
complete range of books and plays
for readers of all ages, ranging from
captivating contemporary stories
to timeless classics. There are three
series, each catering for a different
age group; Young ELI Readers, Teen
ELI Readers and Young Adult ELI
Readers. The books are carefully
edited and beautifully illustrated to
capture the essence of the stories and
plots. The readers are supplemented
with 'Focus on' texts packed with
background cultural information about
the writers and their lives and times.

Mark Twain

The Adventures of
Tom Sawyer

Adaptation and Activities
by Janet Borsbey and Ruth Swan

Illustrated by
Alessandra Vitelli

*For
Isabel Swan,
who shares a birthday
with Mark Twain*

Teen ELI Readers

The Adventures of Tom Sawyer
by Mark Twain
Adaptation and Activities by Janet Borsbey and Ruth Swan
Illustrated by Alessandra Vitelli

The authors would like to thank:
all the team at Eli and E. Chuther

ELI Readers
Founder and Series Editors
Paola Accattoli, Grazia Ancillani, Daniele Garbuglia (Art Director)

Layout
Gianluca Rocchetti

Production Manager
Francesco Capitano

Photo credits
Shutterstock

© 2013 ELI s.r.l.
P.O. Box 6
62019 Recanati (MC)
Italy
T +39 071750701
F +39 071977851
info@elionline.com
www.elionline.com
Typeset in 13 / 18 pt Monotype Dante
Printed in Italy by Tecnostampa Recanati - ERT 233.01
ISBN 9788853615787
First edition: March 2013

www.elireaders.com

Contents

These icons indicate the parts of the story that are recorded

start ▶   stop ■

Aunt Polly
Tom's Aunt.

INTRODUCTION AND MAIN CHARACTERS

Introduction

The story of Tom Sawyer happens in America in about 1840. Tom lives in a small town, in Missouri, near the Mississippi River. The story is about Tom's life – he has a lot of adventures. And it's about his friends.

Tom Sawyer
Tom's mother and father are dead. He lives with his Aunt.

Becky Thatcher
Tom likes Becky a lot.

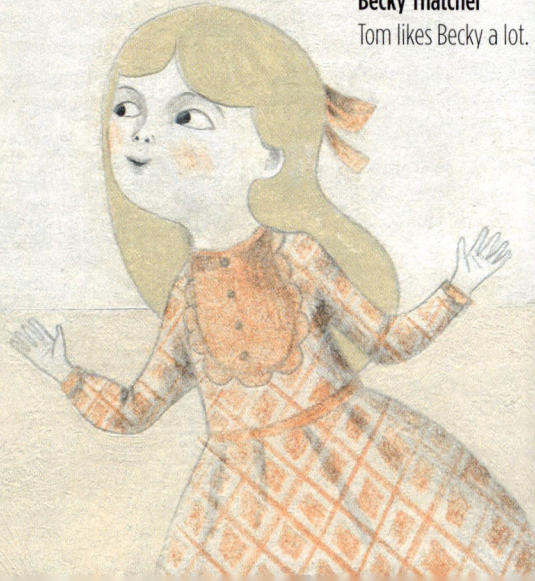

Preface

By the author, Mark Twain

Most of the adventures in this book really happened.
They happened when I was a boy, thirty or forty years ago.
Some of the adventures are things which happened to
me. Some of them happened to my friends.
My book is for children and for adults. I hope it will help
you adults remember; remember when you were a child.

Injun Joe
A very bad man.
People are scared of him.

Huckleberry (Huck) Finn
A poor boy in the town.
He's a friend of Tom's.

Joe Harper
Tom's best friend.

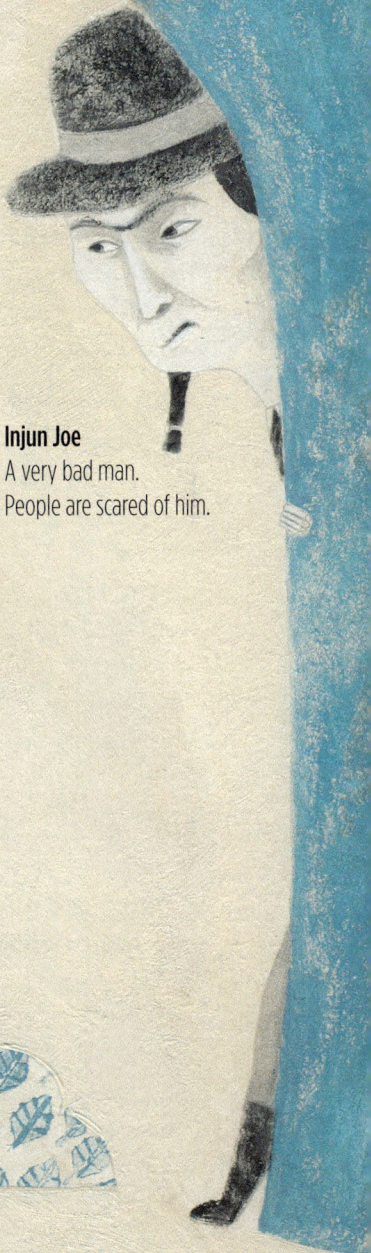

Grammar

1 **Prepositions. Complete the information about Mark Twain, the author of *The Adventures of Tom Sawyer*, with time words from the box.**

> to • in • on • from • in

Mark Twain, the author of *The Adventures of Tom Sawyer*, was born (**1**) __*in*__ 1835. He was actually born (**2**) _____ November 30. He was from Missouri, USA and his real name was Samuel Langhorne Clemens. First of all, he worked as a printer. Then, he worked as a pilot on boats on the Mississippi (**3**) _____ 1857 (**4**) _____ 1861. He met a lot of interesting people of all ages when he was working on the river. Clemens wrote *The Adventures of Tom Sawyer* (**5**) _____ 1876, under the name Mark Twain. The Mississippi is very important to Tom's story.

Vocabulary & Speaking

2a **Match the places from *The Adventures of Tom Sawyer* to their definitions. Use a dictionary to help you.**

1 forest   **a** like Australia, Jamaica and Madagascar
2 island   **b** Fred Flintstone lives in one
3 cave   **c** a place where you find lots of trees
4 river   **d** smaller than a mountain. You can walk up one
5 town   **e** like the Mississippi and the Amazon
6 hill   **f** smaller than a city, but larger than a village

2b **Have you ever visited a cave? Tell your partner about it.**

Vocabulary

3 **Mark Twain doesn't say, but Tom Sawyer is probably a young teenager. What stages of life are the best to do these things?**

When you're a baby   _____

           a child   _____

           a teenager/in your teens   _____

           in your twenties   _____

           in your thirties   _____

           in your fifties   _____

           in your nineties   _____

           _____   _____

---

learn a language • learn to swim • get married • retire
take driving lessons • get a job • travel abroad
learn to fly • have children • leave home

---

4 **In Chapter One, Tom gets into trouble: he goes swimming in the river instead of going to school. What should happen for the bad behaviors below? Write your choice.**

Bad behaviors

1 Missing school _____

2 Being rude to an adult _____

3 Not doing homework _____

4 Using your cell phone in class ____

5 Cheating in a test
(copying/using notes)_____

6 Playing a trick on a teacher _____

7 Being late for school _____

8 Tearing a book _____

- extra chores
- detention (staying longer at school)
- extra homework
- standing outside the classroom
- other

Chapter One

Good Days and Bad Days

▶ 2 "Tom!"

No answer.

"Tom!"

No answer.

"Where *is* that boy? You, Tom!"

No answer.

The old lady took off her glasses. She looked around the room. Then, she looked under the bed, but she only found the cat. Then she heard a noise behind her. She turned around and opened the cupboard door. There was Tom. "Here you are! What are you doing in there, Tom? What's that around your mouth, boy?"

"I don't know, Aunt Polly."

"Well *I* do. It's jam, isn't it? You naughty boy! What am I going to do with you? Where's my stick★?"

"Look behind you, Aunt!" said Tom, quickly.

She looked behind her. Tom ran out of the door and jumped over the fence★. He was free.

stick – ⌐___

fence – like a wall, a fence is often made of wood (picture page 15)

Tom's aunt laughed. "He's done that to me a thousand times. I still haven't learnt! Grrr! I'll have him* when he comes home! He's my poor dead sister's boy. I want to make him a good boy. I feel bad if I hit him and bad if I don't. But I have to punish* him. So, what can I do with him? I can make him work. He can work for me on Saturday."

It was a hot afternoon. Tom didn't want to go back to school. So, he decided to go swimming in the river. When he got home, Aunt Polly was waiting for him. "Was it very hot in school this afternoon, Tom?" she said.

"Yes, Aunt. It was very hot."

"But you didn't go to school. You went swimming in the river!" said Sid, Tom's brother. "Look, your shirt's wet."

"Why did you do that, Sid? Now, I'll get into trouble*! I'll have you for that, Sid!" said Tom. Then, before Aunt Polly could catch him, he ran out of the house.

Aunt Polly was now sure about Tom's punishment. "No free time for Tom on Saturday. He can work for me."

to have someone – (here) to say you will do something bad to someone
to punish – (noun = punishment) if you do something wrong, sometimes the teacher punishes you
to get into trouble – to have problems because you do something wrong

Tom was free again. He went to find his friends. On his way down the street, he met a stranger*. The boy was a little bit taller than Tom. The boy was wearing city clothes. He was wearing shoes, but it wasn't Sunday. The boy looked at Tom. Tom's clothes were old. Tom wasn't wearing any shoes. The boy didn't like Tom. Tom didn't like the boy.

"What's your name?" said Tom.

"I'm not telling you," the stranger answered.

"Then I'll fight you!" said Tom.

"And I'll fight you too, but I'll win!"

Then the stranger jumped on Tom and they started fighting. Soon, Tom was sitting on the boy. "Say 'enough' and tell me your name!" said Tom.

"No!"

"Say 'enough' and tell me your name!" said Tom, again.

"All right! My name's Alfred Temple. Now enough!" said the boy.

Tom stood up. Alfred, the stranger, escaped* down the street.

Tom got home quite late that night. He quietly climbed through the window. He didn't want to get

stranger – someone you don't know
to escape – to get away and to be free

into more trouble. But Aunt Polly was waiting for him. "Tom! Look at your clothes! What did you do to them? They're all dirty. You've torn* your shirt! And look at your face! What *am* I going to do with you? Well, you can paint my fence on Saturday. *That's* what you can do!"

★★★

Saturday arrived. It was a beautiful day. Tom went out into the garden. He had a bucket* of white paint and a brush. He looked at the fence. It was very long. He didn't want to work. He wanted to go swimming. He wanted to have fun with his friends. He put his brush into the paint and started work. "I hope my friends don't see me," he thought. "They'll laugh at me."

Then, Tom had an idea. And it was a *wonderful* idea.

Tom's friend, Ben Rogers, came along the road. Tom pretended* not to see him. Tom continued painting. Then, Ben saw Tom. "Hey!" he said. "What are you doing? Why are you working on a *Saturday?* Don't you want to come swimming?"

"*Work?* Oh, this isn't *work*," said Tom. "I've never painted a fence before. I like it. It's not *work*, it's *fun*."

---

to tear – (tore/torn) to pull clothes or paper into pieces

bucket –
to pretend – to act in a way which isn't true

Ben watched Tom. Tom looked very happy. Ben thought for a moment, then he said, "Can I paint a bit of fence, Tom? Please? I'll give you my half of my apple."

Tom continued to paint. Then Ben said, "I'll give you *all* of my apple!"

Tom agreed. He gave Ben the brush and the bucket of paint. Ben started painting. Tom sat under a tree and ate his apple. A little while later, some more of Tom's friends came along the road. All of them wanted to paint the fence. At the end of the morning, Tom had a lot of treasure★! Four wonderful marbles★, some blue glass, a part of a knife, a key, a fish-hook★ and half a piece of the teacher's chalk★. He was rich!

Tom went to find Aunt Polly. "Can I go and have fun now, Aunt?"

"What do you mean? You have to finish painting the fence before you can go."

"But I've finished, Aunt. Can I go and have fun?"

"Finished? But that's impossible. Show me."

Aunt Polly went outside. She saw the fence. It was beautiful. She couldn't believe it. "Well yes, Tom. That's a good job. You can go and play now."

treasure –

marble – a coloured glass ball. You can play games with marbles

fish-hook –

chalk – teachers often use chalk to write with. It's white

Tom ran out into the street. He was free!

It was time for the usual Saturday fight. Tom was the leader of his gang*. Tom's best friend, Joe Harper, was the leader in another gang. It was time to fight.

The fight was wonderful. At the end, the two leaders counted all the dead. They counted all the prisoners*. "What a good fight! What a good day! See you all next Saturday!" everyone said.

Everyone went home. Tom was smiling. On the way home, he walked past Jeff Thatcher's house. There was a new girl in the garden. She was pretty. In fact, Tom thought she was *very* pretty. She was an angel*. She was even prettier than Amy Lawrence. Tom forgot all about Amy Lawrence.

Tom pretended not to see this angel. He walked up and down in front of her garden. He walked like a man. He acted like a man. He wanted this beautiful girl to see him. He showed off* as much as he could. After a while, she threw a flower. Then she ran inside her house. The flower was for Tom. He looked around. No-one saw him. He picked up the flower and put it in his pocket. It was wonderful. He walked home. He was smiling from ear to ear. Who was she? Who was this angel?

gang – (here) a group of friends
prisoner – a person who isn't free
angel – (here) a very beautiful person

to show off – to act so that people will look at you

When he got home, Sid was in the garden. Tom picked up a stone. He threw it at Sid. *Yes*!

"Ouch!" said Sid. "Why did you do that?"

"You always want me to be in trouble. It's not fair*!" said Tom.

At dinner time, Sid dropped a plate on the floor. "Tom did that!" said Sid.

Aunt Polly picked up her stick. She hit Tom.

"Hey, Aunt Polly. That's not fair! Don't hit *me*! It was *Sid*, not *me*!"

Aunt Polly looked surprised. Then she said, "Well, you probably did something bad today, anyway. You're always getting into trouble."

Tom went outside. He was angry and miserable*. It wasn't fair. He went to find his angel. Outside her house, he threw some stones at a window. After a while, someone opened it. Tom looked up, but he wasn't quick enough. Someone threw a bucket of water. It went all over him.

"What a horrible day. It really isn't fair. Life isn't fair," thought Tom.

He went home, took off his wet clothes and went to bed.

fair – (here) right
miserable – very sad

Stop & Check

1 **Are these statements true (T) or false (F)? Correct the false statements.**

	T	F
1 Tom lives with his aunt and his sister.	☐	☑
2 Tom loves swimming.	☐	☐
3 Tom's punishment is to paint the fence.	☐	☐
4 Tom paints the fence while his friends watch.	☐	☐
5 The new girl in town is called Amy Lawrence.	☐	☐
6 Tom gets into trouble because of Sid.	☐	☐
7 Aunt Polly punishes Sid for dropping a plate.	☐	☐

Glossary Work

2 **Tom's Treasure. Can you work out how much treasure Tom got from his friends?**

1 Tom has 2 times 5 pieces of chalk = ___ pieces of chalk.

2 Tom has 2 times as many pieces of blue glass as he has marbles = ___ pieces of blue glass.

3 Tom has 8 fewer marbles than apples = ___ marbles.

4 Tom has ½ as many fish-hooks as he has marbles = ___ fish-hooks.

5 Tom has 8 more apples than pieces of chalk = ___ apples.

6 How many things did Tom get from his friends? ___

Reading for Key

3 **Read the sentences about swimming. Choose the best word (A, B or C) for each space.**

1 Tom ___*went*___ swimming yesterday.

    A went   **B** go   **C** goes

2 Tom _____ swimming on hot days.

    A wants   **B** likes   **C** plays

3 The river is _____ the town.

    A near   **B** far   **C** back

4 There isn't _____ swimming pool in the town.

    A a   **B** the   **C** some

5 Amy _____ like swimming in the river.

    A don't   **B** never   **C** doesn't

6 They all have races to find the _____ swimmer.

    A fast   **B** fastest   **C** fasting

Before-reading Activity

Vocabulary

4a Tick the adjectives which best describe Tom Sawyer.

- ☐ naughty
- ☐ clever
- ☐ unkind
- ☐ sporty
- ☐ funny
- ☐ hard-working
- ☐ normal
- ☐ popular
- ☐ quiet
- ☐ sweet

4b Think about Tom's character. What do you think he does in Chapter Two. Choose the best option. Then read Chapter Two and check your answers.

1 ☐ **A** Tom is interested in a lesson.

    ☐ **B** Tom is bored by a lesson.

2 ☐ **A** Tom sits next to his angel at school.

    ☐ **B** Tom sits next to the teacher at school.

3 ☐ **A** Tom meets one of his friends at 11.30 pm.

    ☐ **B** Tom meets one of his friends at 10.00 am.

4 ☐ **A** Tom dreams about his angel.

    ☐ **B** Tom dreams about a dead body.

Chapter Two

Church on Sunday, School on Monday

▶ 3 It was Sunday morning. Time for Sunday-school*
and church. Aunt Polly tested Tom on his bible
lesson. Tom couldn't remember any of it. Mary,
Tom's cousin, helped him. She was kind and patient,
so, in the end, Tom learnt most of it. Then he put
on his best clothes and his shoes. He hated wearing
shoes. It was too hot to wear shoes. Then he went
off to Sunday-school. On the way, Tom met his
friend, Bill. "Hey, Bill! Have you got a yellow ticket?"

"Yes, I have."

"I'll buy it from you. What do you want? I'll give
you some marbles and a fishing-pole*."

"Ok."

Then Tom bought some tickets from some of
his other friends. He got three red tickets, another
yellow one and quite a few blue ones. If you had
enough tickets, you could get a prize* from the
Sunday-school teacher. To get a blue ticket, you had
to remember two pieces from the bible. Ten blue

Sunday-school – lessons on Sunday to learn about religion
fishing-pole – the long piece of wood that you use to catch fish
prize – a present. You get it if you do something good

tickets were the same as one red one. Ten red tickets were the same as one yellow one. For ten yellow tickets, there was a prize. But to win the prize, you had to learn two thousand pieces from the bible. Only the older students ever won the prize. The prize, of course, was a new bible.

"Now everyone. I want you to sit up straight. Face me and listen carefully," said Mr. Walters, the teacher.

It was the same every Sunday. It was very boring. Tom and his friends didn't listen. They played and whispered★ to each other.

While the teacher was talking, some visitors came into the church. Everyone started whispering some more. It was unusual to have visitors in town. They were with Jeff Thatcher's father. One was a tall important-looking man. Then, there was a woman and a young girl. Mr. Walters showed them the best seats. Tom couldn't believe it; the little girl was his angel.

Mr. Walters introduced the visitors to the Sunday-school pupils. The tall man was a judge★. A very important person. He came from Constantinople. That was *twelve miles*★ away! His name was Judge

to whisper – to speak very, very quietly
judge – if you steal something, a judge will decide what to do with you
miles – 1 mile is a little more than 1½ kilometers (1.609 kilometers)

Thatcher. Suddenly, all the pupils became very quiet and very good. Then Tom stood up. He slowly walked up to the front of the church. Everyone was watching him. He gave Mr. Walters nine yellow tickets, nine red ones and ten blue ones. Mr. Walters was very, *very* surprised, but he was also very pleased. He wanted to show off to Judge Thatcher. He wanted Judge Thatcher to see his wonderful pupils. Mr. Walters gave Tom his prize – a new bible. Judge Thatcher was looking. But more importantly, so was his daughter, Tom's angel, Becky Thatcher. Tom felt wonderful. Then Judge Thatcher spoke to him. "Congratulations, Thomas. You've worked very hard. You know a lot about the bible. You've learned two thousand pieces from it. Well done. So, Thomas, I want to ask you a question."

"Yes, Judge. What is it?" said Tom quietly.

"What's your favorite story in the bible? Can you tell me?"

Tom looked at the floor. He didn't say anything. He didn't know what to say. "What *is* my favorite bible story?" he thought. "I don't know! What can I say to the judge?"

"The poor boy's shy," said Mrs. Thatcher. "I know you'll tell *me*, Thomas. So, your favorite bible story is …."

"ROMEO AND JULIET!" said Tom loudly.

★★★

It was Monday morning and Tom was miserable. Another week of school. On his way to school, Tom met Huckleberry Finn. Huckleberry didn't have to go to school. He didn't have to go to church. His father was lazy and didn't work. People in the town didn't like Huckleberry's father. Huckleberry was very poor. But, all the boys in the town liked Huckleberry. They wanted to be like him.

"Hello, Huck. What have you got there?" said Tom.

"An old shoe. I'm going to bury★ it in the grave-yard★, tonight. I have to go at midnight and I have to say a prayer★. I've got a bad toe. Old Mrs. Hopkins says that'll make my toe better."

"Can I come, too?"

"Of course you can, if you want to. I'll come to your house tonight. I'll make a noise like a cat outside your window. Then we can go together."

to bury – to put something in the ground and cover it
grave-yard – a place where you put dead people in the ground
prayer – (verb = to pray) to talk to your God

Mark Twain

Tom was late for school. The teacher punished him. He told him to sit with the girls. Tom was really pleased. The only free seat was next to his angel, Becky Thatcher. At first, she pretended not to look at him. Then he put an apple next to her. "Take it. I've got more," he whispered.

Then he drew a picture for her. She liked it. "Can you teach me to draw?" she whispered back to him.

"Of course!" said Tom. He was delighted*.

***

That night, at about half past eleven, Tom heard a cat outside his bedroom window. "Huck!" he thought.

He got out of bed very quietly. He climbed out of the window. "Meow-meow." he called.

Huck answered, "Meow-meow."

The boys quietly went to the grave-yard. "Have you got the shoe?" whispered Tom.

"Yes, here it is," said Huck. "Now let's start digging*!"

The boys began to dig. Then, suddenly, Tom heard something. "Shh! I think there's someone here," he said. "Yes, I can hear voices. Quick, let's hide!"

delighted – very happy
to dig – to make a hole in the ground

24

Tom and Huck hid behind a tree. They were very quiet. In the dark, they could see three men: Dr. Robinson, Muff Potter and Injun Joe. At first, Muff Potter and Injun Joe were digging, but then they stopped. Dr. Robinson was angry. "I paid you a lot of money to do this job for me. I need this man's body for my medical research. Do the job!"

"No! We want more money. You didn't give us enough. Give us more money!" said Injun Joe.

The doctor picked up a big stick and tried to hit Injun Joe. The doctor hit Muff Potter, by mistake, and Potter fell down. Injun Joe quickly took Muff Potter's knife. He ran towards the doctor. The next minute, the doctor was dead. Injun Joe looked in the doctor's pockets. He took all the doctor's money and his gold watch. Potter was still lying on the ground. Then, Joe put the knife in Potter's hand. A short time later, Potter woke up. "What happened?" he said.

"You killed the doctor," said Injun Joe. "That's what happened. You're a murderer*!"

Potter was very confused. "But I don't remember anything. My head hurts. Oh, no! What have I done?"

murderer – a killer

Huck and Tom were really scared. They ran away as fast as possible. They ran until they couldn't run any more. Then they made a promise*. They promised never to tell anyone.

***

The following day, everyone was talking about it. "Have you heard the news? Muff Potter killed the doctor last night! They found Potter's knife next to the body. Injun Joe saw it all. He says Muff Potter's a murderer."

The news went around the village very quickly. Soon the sheriff* arrived with Muff Potter. Potter looked very scared. There were lots of people there. Everyone was shouting at him. The sheriff took Muff Potter to jail*. Tom and Huck didn't know what to do.

For the next few nights, Tom had horrible dreams; dreams about blood and murder. Tom was worried. He was worried about Muff Potter. He knew that Injun Joe was the real murderer. He was too scared to tell anyone. Huck was scared too. The boys felt bad about Muff. Every day, they went to the jail. They gave Muff things to eat and drink. Tom and Huck wanted to help him.

promise – (verb = to promise) a thing you say that you will definitely do
sheriff – a type of police officer
jail – a place where you go if you steal something

After-reading Activities

Stop & Check

1 Put the events from Chapter Two into the order they appear in the text.

- ☐ Huckleberry Finn and Tom meet late at night
- ☐ Injun Joe kills Dr. Robinson
- ☐ Judge Thatcher and his family come into the church
- ☐ Then, the boys go to the grave-yard
- ☐ Tom buys tickets from his friends
- ☑ Tom goes off to Sunday-school
- ☐ Tom pretends that he has learned a lot from the bible
- ☐ Injun Joe, Muff Potter and Dr. Robinson argue

Characters

2 Which adjectives can you use to describe the following people? Use words from the box. You can use the words more than once.

> pretty • poor • free • unkind
>
> important • lazy • clever • tall

1 Tom _____

2 Tom's brother, Sid _____

3 Becky Thatcher _____

4 Judge Thatcher _____

5 Huck _____

6 Huck's father _____

Grammar

3 **Adjectives give more information about people and things. Adverbs give more information about how things happen. Choose an adjective or adverb to complete the sentences.**

1 "Face me and listen ___carefully___," said Mr. Walters.
careful/carefully

2 Tom sat next to Becky. He was very _____.
happy/happily

3 Huck had a _____ toe. bad/badly

4 They went _____ to the grave-yard. quick/quickly

5 Mary helped Tom _____. patient/patiently

6 "Can you help me to draw?" asked Becky _____.
quiet/quietly

Before-reading Activity

Listening

▶ 4 **4a** **Listen to the first part of Chapter Three. Are these statements true (T) or false (F)? Tick the correct box.**

		T	F
1	Tom is in school.	✓	☐
2	Becky Thatcher is in school, as usual.	☐	☐
3	The girls say that Becky is sick.	☐	☐
4	Aunt Polly is worried about Tom.	☐	☐
5	Tom isn't worried about Becky.	☐	☐
6	Tom is happy; he shows off to Becky.	☐	☐
7	Becky is unkind to Tom.	☐	☐
8	Tom thinks that no-one loves him.	☐	☐

4b **Now read Chapter Three and check your answers.**

Chapter Three

Pirates in a Storm

4 "Where *is* Becky Thatcher?" Tom thought. "She wasn't in school yesterday, or the day before. She's not in school today. Where is she?"

During recess, he heard some of the girls talking. "Becky's sick. I went to see her yesterday," said Amy Lawrence.

After school, Tom walked past Becky's house. The curtains were closed. Everything was quiet. He was really miserable. "I hope she gets better soon. I don't want her to die. I love her."

At home, Tom was very quiet at dinner. Aunt Polly was worried about him. "Are you sick, Tom?" she asked.

Tom didn't answer. He just looked sad. "I hope Becky gets better," he thought.

Every day in school, Tom waited outside. He looked for Becky. All the girls came, but Becky didn't. Tom was miserable. Then, one day, Tom was waiting as usual. There she was! The last girl to come was Becky. Tom was delighted. He showed off as much as possible. He did everything he could. He ran, he jumped, he climbed a tree. "Look at me, Becky! Look at me!" Tom thought.

But Becky didn't look at him. She pretended he wasn't there. "Some boys really show off. I think they're very stupid," she said to one of her friends.

Tom felt horrible. He was miserable. "Nobody loves me," he said to himself. "I'm never coming back to school again. I'm going to run away*."

5   A little later, he met his best friend, Joe. Joe wanted to run away too. "My mother punished me, but it wasn't fair. She doesn't love me. Nobody loves me," said Joe.

"Then let's run away together," said Tom. "We can be pirates. We can capture* a boat. We'll go to Jackson's Island. We'll make a camp near the forest. Let's meet at midnight. Bring some food. Bring your fishing-pole."

"Yes, and let's get Huck. He can come too."

Tom and Joe went to find Huck. "We're going to be pirates. We're going to capture a boat. We're going to make a pirate camp on Jackson's Island. Do you want to come too?"

to run away – to go away from home without telling anyone
to capture – (here) to take something from someone

Huck agreed. He liked adventure, too.

★★★

The pirates met at midnight. It was their favorite time of night. Tom had some ham. Joe had some cheese and bread. They went down to the river. There was Huck, waiting for them. In the river, there was a small, old fishing-boat. The pirates captured it and went off to Jackson's Island. There, they made a pirate camp. They made a fire and told pirate stories. Then, finally, they all went to sleep.

The boys woke up late the following morning. They went swimming and then they caught some fish. They cooked the fish over the fire. They had a wonderful lunch. In the afternoon, Tom heard a noise in the distance. It was the sound of a large gun*. "That means somebody's lost in the water," said Tom. "You hear the gun when someone gets lost in the river."

Then they saw a ferry-boat*. There were a lot of townspeople* on the ferry-boat. They were looking in the water.

"Perhaps it's Injun Joe," said Huck. "Perhaps he's lost in the water."

gun –
ferry-boat – like a bus, but on the water
townspeople – people from the town

"I hope so," said Tom.

"I don't think it's Injun Joe," said Joe. "I think they're looking for us!"

The boys thought this was wonderful. *They* were lost and the whole town was looking for them. "*Now* they're all sorry. *Now* their hearts are breaking. We're pirates lost at sea!" they said.

The three lost pirates spent the afternoon talking about the townspeople. They guessed what people were saying. They were famous. They were heroes*. The boys were delighted.

In the evening, they caught some fish and cooked it on the fire. They ate their supper quietly. They were all thinking. They were thinking about home. They began to feel sorry. Then Joe said, "What do you think? Can we go home?"

"We're pirates. Of course we can't go home!" said Tom.

Huck agreed. But, secretly, Tom and Huck agreed with Joe. They missed home too. "Perhaps Aunt Polly is sad," thought Tom. "I need to find out. I'll find out tonight."

hero – (here) a very good and very famous person

He waited until Joe and Huck were asleep. Then he quietly left the camp. He got to the river. He walked as far as possible, then he started swimming. When he got to the town, he went back to his house. He looked through the window. Aunt Polly was there. So was Joe's mother. They were crying. They were talking about the boys. They were talking about the funeral*. "Tom was a good boy, really," said Aunt Polly. "He did some bad things. But all boys sometimes do bad things. He had a kind heart."

"I know. My Joe was the same," said Mrs. Harper. "They were good boys."

"Yes, Saturday will be a horrible day," said Aunt Polly.

And they both started crying again. Tom was sorry for them. "I must tell the others," he thought. "We all need to come home. But we need to have a plan. I'll go back to the camp. I'll tell the boys."

***

The next day, the boys swam and fished as usual. Joe was quiet and sad. He wanted to go home. Huck was sad too. He missed his life in the town. Tom told

funeral – when people come to say goodbye to someone who is dead, this is the funeral

them to wait. "We need to make a plan. I've got an idea, but we need to wait."

That night, Joe woke up at midnight. "Huck! Tom! I think there's a storm coming!"

Joe was right. The wind was getting stronger and stronger. The boys ran out of their tent.

"Come on you two. It's not safe in here," said Tom.

"Yes, we need to find somewhere safe. Somewhere away from the rain," said Huck.

The boys ran into the forest. They went to hide under some trees. The storm was terrible. The wind was very strong. It was raining and raining. The boys couldn't see anything. The noise of the storm was very loud. They couldn't hear each other. They were cold and very scared.

When the storm stopped, the boys went back to their camp. There was nothing there. "We nearly died here," said Joe. "Look, there's nothing here. The tent has gone. *Everything* has gone. I think it's time to go home. Come on Tom. Huck agrees with me. Tell us your plan and then we can go home."

"We need to wait, boys," said Tom. "We need to wait until Saturday. Two nights ago, I went back to town. I was worried about Aunt Polly. I saw Aunt Polly and Joe's mother. They were talking about our funeral."

Then, Tom told his friends about his secret plan. Everyone agreed, it was a really good idea. ■

Stop & Check

1 **Correct the mistakes in the summary of Chapter Three. There are seven mistakes.**

When Aunt Polly is sick at home, Tom is very worried about her. When Becky comes back to school, she isn't very kind to Tom. Tom decides to run away. His friend, Joe, doesn't want to run away. They go to New York with Huck. They pretend that they are cowboys and camp on the island. They have fun at first, but then they start to think about home. Huck goes back to town. He hears Aunt Polly talking with Joe's mother about the boys' weddings. When Tom gets back to the bus, there is a terrible storm. The boys agree to go home.

Grammar

2 **Irregular Verbs Wordsearch. Find the past tense of the verbs in the wordsearch and complete the sentences.**

1 Becky ___was___ (be) ill.
2 "I hope Becky gets better," _____ (think) Tom.
3 Tom _____ (feel) horrible.
4 The pirates _____ (meet) at midnight.
5 They _____ (go) to the river.
6 The boys _____ (wake up) late in the morning.
7 Joe _____ (catch) some fish.
8 The boys _____ (see) a ferry-boat.
9 There _____ (be) a lot of townspeople on the ferry-boat.
10 They _____ (eat) their supper, quietly.
11 They _____ (begin) to feel sorry.

B	F	W	O	K	E	U	P
M	E	T	C	O	C	L	W
A	L	G	W	K	A	W	E
W	T	S	A	W	U	E	R
D	D	E	S	N	G	N	E
T	H	O	U	G	H	T	X
B	E	L	R	N	T	E	A

Writing for Key

3 **Read the information about the river trip and part of a letter to Judge Thatcher. Fill in the information in Judge Thatcher's notes.**

My dear brother,
I hope you are all well. We are here. We had a wonderful trip to Jackson's Island on Sunday. We went on the Mississippi Queen, a fine old ferry-boat. You should take Becky there, I'm sure she'd love it. The trip on the boat is fun - it takes about ninety minutes to get to the island. It's not expensive either: fifty cents for an adult and that's for a return trip.

Jackson's Island Ferry-boat

* * * * * * * * * * * * * * * * *
**Tuesday - Sunday
8.30 am
Children free**
* * * * * * * * * * * * * * * * *

Judge Thatcher's notes:

Name of river: _Mississippi_
Name of ferry-boat: _____
Leaving time: _____

Day(s): _____
Duration of journey: _____
Cost per person (return trip): _____

Before-reading Activity

Speaking

4 **Look at some events from the Chapter Four. Discuss the questions in pairs.**

1 *Everyone goes to the boys' funeral.*
How do people feel?

2 *The boys go back home.*
What do people do when they see them?

3 *Tom is angry with Becky.*
What does he do?

4 *Becky is angry with Tom.*
What does she do?

Chapter Four

Tom and Becky

6 It was Saturday. It was a beautiful day, but everyone in the town was miserable. It was the day of the funeral. Everyone went to the church. Becky Thatcher was there. She was crying. "Why was I so horrible to Tom? Why did I pretend he wasn't there? I loved him and now he's gone! I'll never forget you, Tom."

One by one, people from the town got up to speak. They all said kind things about the boys. Everyone was sorry.

Then, in the middle of the funeral, the church door opened. It opened very, very slowly. Everyone at the back of the church started whispering. Everyone stood up and looked at the door. First, Tom came in. Then came Joe. Finally, Huck walked into the church. Aunt Polly ran to Tom. She hugged* him and kissed him. Becky Thatcher stopped crying. Mrs. Harper, Joe's mother, hugged and kissed all three boys. Judge

to hug – to take someone in your arms in a nice way

40

Thatcher and his wife smiled. Even the Sunday-school teacher smiled. Everyone was delighted.

So *that* was Tom's secret plan; for the pirates to go to their own funerals. Now they weren't in trouble. Everyone was too happy to see them.

★★★

Tom, Joe and Huck were heroes. Everyone in school wanted to talk to them. Everyone wanted to hear about their adventure. They told everyone about fishing and swimming. They told everyone about the terrible storm. They were famous.

Becky Thatcher now *wanted* Tom to look at her. Now she *wanted* Tom to talk to her. She was sorry. But Tom pretended she wasn't there. *He* talked to Amy Lawrence. Becky was sad and angry. So, during recess, *she* talked to Alfred Temple. Poor Alfred. Becky only talked to Alfred because she wanted Tom to feel bad. Tom pretended he didn't care*. But, secretly, he felt bad too. Alfred was really happy. Becky Thatcher was *his* girl now.

At lunchtime, Tom went home. He didn't want to see Alfred and Becky together. Becky was soon

to care – (here) to worry, to feel bad

bored with Alfred. Tom wasn't there to see her. She couldn't make Tom feel bad. Poor Alfred Temple. Becky left Alfred and she went away to talk to her friends. Now *Alfred* was hurt and angry. "I hope Tom gets into big trouble! It's not fair."

***

The teacher, Mr. Dobbins, didn't want to be a teacher. He wanted to be a doctor. But he came from a poor family. He didn't have enough money to go to college. Mr. Dobbins had a beautiful, big book in his desk. He loved that book. Every day, when his pupils were reading, he took his book out of his desk. He studied it hard. When it was time to go, he put the book back. He always took the key away. Everyone had lots of ideas about the book. But really, no-one knew what was in it.

That afternoon, Becky went back into the schoolroom. She walked past the desk. The key was there! This was her chance. She opened the desk and looked at the book: *Professor someone's Anatomy*. The name didn't help. She turned some more pages. Suddenly, behind her, she heard a noise.

"What are you doing there, Becky?" said Tom.

Becky jumped. "Oh Tom. Why did you come in so quietly? Now look! I've torn Mr. Dobbins' book! I'll be in big trouble."

Tom was pleased. Becky was being horrible to him. He wanted her to be in trouble.

Everyone came back into the schoolroom. Mr. Dobbins came in. Everyone got out their books. They all started reading. Mr. Dobbins opened his desk. Then he opened his book and he saw the torn page. He looked very, very angry. Becky was looking very scared. Everyone was quiet. No-one said anything. Then Mr. Dobbins spoke. "I can always find you. You know I can. So, did you tear this book, Benjamin Rogers?"

"No, I didn't."

"Joseph Harper, did you?"

Another no. Then another no and another. Mr. Dobbins started asking the girls. First, he asked Amy Lawrence. Then he asked Gracie Miller and Susan Harper. The next girl was Becky Thatcher. Tom looked at Becky. She looked very scared. Mr.

Dobbins looked at Becky. "Rebecca Thatcher, did you tear this book?"

Suddenly, Tom jumped up. "*I* tore it, Mr. Dobbins. *I* did it."

No-one could believe it, especially Becky. She looked at Tom, lovingly. Tom didn't care about his punishment. He was happy that Becky loved him again.

★★★

It was nearly time for the summer vacation. Mr. Dobbins was always horrible near vacation time. The end of school meant the school show. Everyone had to learn a poem or part of a story. Every year, at the end of the show, Mr. Dobbins got up to speak. All the people in the town came to watch.

Mr. Dobbins wanted everyone to do well. The younger boys always had trouble. The stories and poems were difficult to learn. They made lots of mistakes. Mr. Dobbins made them stay after school. He was horrible to them, so they hated the school show.

One day, during recess, the younger boys were talking together.

"I hate the school show. Dobby's always horrible to us."

"I know. I can never remember my poem. He's made me stay after school three times this week."

"Me too. Last week I had to stay every day! He's really horrible, isn't he?"

"Well, let's do something about it!"

"But what can we do?"

"Let's all think about it. Perhaps we'll have an idea."

After school, the boys all met together.

"Has anyone got any ideas?"

"Yes, I have. I've got an idea, let's play a trick on him."

"Yes! Let's play a trick on Dobby. And I know what we'll do. We need some gold paint!"

Reading for Key

1 **Read the first part of Chapter Four again. Are the sentences *right* (A) or *wrong* (B)? Choose *doesn't say* (C), if there isn't enough information in the text to answer (A) or (B).**

1 It was Sunday morning.
  A Right **B** Wrong **C** Doesn't say

2 Everyone in the town was very sad.
  A Right **B** Wrong **C** Doesn't say

3 Becky Thatcher brought flowers to the church.
  A Right **B** Wrong **C** Doesn't say

4 Joe was the first boy to come into the church.
  A Right **B** Wrong **C** Doesn't say

5 Aunt Polly was angry with Tom.
  A Right **B** Wrong **C** Doesn't say

6 The Sunday-school teacher was happy to see the boys.
  A Right **B** Wrong **C** Doesn't say

Vocabulary & Speaking

2a **Find the odd one out in each group. Write why. Your answer can be different from other people's answers.**

1 volleyball (tennis) soccer basketball
  because you need a racket to play tennis

2 swimming running skiing cycling

3 ice hockey skiing skating diving

4 basketball windsurfing table tennis water polo

5 cycling baseball football soccer

2b Talk in pairs about your favorite sports.

Grammar

3a Past Simple. Put the irregular verbs into the sentences below.

1 "You ___went___ swimming!" **go**
2 Tom _____ out of the door. **run**
3 Ben _____, "Can I paint a bit of the fence?" **say**
4 Aunt Polly picked up her stick. She _____ Tom. **hit**
5 He _____ off his wet clothes and went to bed. **take**

3b Put the questions into the right order.

1 go/did/Where/you _____Where did you go_____ ?
2 that jam/get/Where/you/did _____?
3 you/did/How/the island/get to _____?
4 Why/you/this book/did/tear _____?
5 this/When/do/you/did _____?

Before-reading Activity

Speaking

4 In Chapter Five, the boys play their trick on Mr. Dobbins. Work in pairs to discuss the questions.

1 What do you think they will do with the gold paint?
2 Have you ever played a trick on someone?
   If yes, what did you do?
   If no, would you like to play a trick on someone?
3 Are there any problems with playing tricks on people?

Chapter Five

The Summer Vacation

▶7 Mr. Dobbins was bald*. He didn't like being bald. He often wore a hat to hide his bald head. Sometimes, when it was hot in school, Mr. Dobbins took his hat off. He looked funny without his hat.

The night of the school show came. One by one, Mr. Dobbins' pupils said their poems and stories. Some of the older pupils said things in Latin and Greek. Becky's poem was perfect. Even Tom was surprised at himself. He remembered the whole of his poem. He was very happy, so was Aunt Polly. Then, it was time for Mr. Dobbins to speak.

Mr. Dobbins stood up and started speaking. It was very boring, but he loved speaking. "Ladies and gentlemen. I hope you enjoyed our show. All my pupils worked very hard ..."

Some of the townspeople started to go to sleep. Then, high above Mr. Dobbins, Ben Rogers opened a window. Slowly; very, very slowly, Ben put his fishing-pole through the window. His fish-hook

bald – without any hair

came down. It came down slowly; very, very slowly. Mr. Dobbins was still speaking. "… and, in the next school year …"

Ben's fish-hook came nearer and nearer. Everyone in the room started whispering. All the people in the room were watching it.

"… the new geography books have been …"

Very, very slowly, Ben's fish-hook came nearer and nearer to Mr. Dobbins' hat.

"Now!" whispered Joe. "Do it now!"

Then, very quickly, Ben caught Mr. Dobbins' hat. And he pulled it off. All the people in the room started laughing. They laughed and laughed. There was Mr. Dobbins' bald head. And on Mr. Dobbins' bald head, there was a ring of gold paint. His head had a ring of gold!

★★★

Tom was bored. The summer vacation was long. Becky was away in Constantinople with Judge Thatcher. There was nothing to do. There were some birthday parties, but not very many. The circus came to town. Then it went away the next day. The boys played circus for a while. Then they were all bored. Tom decided to write a diary. He decided to write about his vacation. He decided to write about all his adventures. Nothing happened for three days. There was nothing to write. So, Tom stopped. He was bored.

Then Tom was sick.

Tom was very sick. He went to bed. He was hot and then he was cold. He couldn't see anyone. He couldn't hear anyone. Aunt Polly was worried. Cousin Mary was worried. Even Sid was worried. Tom's friends came to see him. They were all worried, too.

"Is Tom going to die?" said Joe.

"I don't know, Joe," said Aunt Polly. "I don't know."

"Please don't die, Tom!" said Huck. "You're my best friend in the world."

Joe, Ben and all Tom's friends prayed for him. "We'll never be bad again. Please live, Tom!" they all said.

Even Huck prayed for Tom. Huck didn't really

know how to pray, but even Huck prayed. He
prayed for Tom to get well.

★★★

Ben, Joe and Huck waited for news. They went
to see Aunt Polly every day. But they couldn't see
Tom. "When can we see Tom?" said Joe.

"I don't know," said Aunt Polly. "He's still
very sick."

Yes, Tom was *very* sick. For two weeks, the
doctor came every day. He looked worried. Then,
one day, Tom slowly opened his eyes. "Why are
you here?" he said.

"Hello, Tom. You're sick. But I think you're
going to get better now," said the doctor.

Aunt Polly was delighted. So were all Tom's
friends. Ben, Joe and Huck visited Tom. They
brought him some apples and grapes. They were
all really happy. "We all prayed for you," said Joe.
"Even Huck prayed for you."

"Huck prayed?" Tom was very surprised.

Finally, after three weeks in bed, Tom was able to
go outside. He didn't feel very strong and he felt tired.

"Don't go swimming!" said Aunt Polly. "I don't want you to be sick again."

Tom agreed. He didn't want to be sick again, either.

He went to find his friends. He found Joe and Huck. They were fishing. "Hey, Tom! You're here!" said Huck.

"Hooray! Come on. Let's go swimming!" said Joe.

"I can't. I don't want to get sick again."

"Then go and get your fishing-pole," said Huck. "This is a really good place. We've caught three fish already."

Tom was really happy. It was good to be with his friends again.

★★★

It was nearly time for Muff Potter's day in the courtroom*. All the townspeople were talking about it. Tom didn't like listening to them. He couldn't sleep. He thought about Injun Joe. He was worried and scared. "I hope Huck hasn't told anyone about that night," he thought. "I'll ask him, then I'll feel better."

courtroom – see picture on page 63

Tom and Huck went to a quiet place together. "Have you told anyone about *that*?" said Tom.

"About what?"

"You know what."

"Oh, *that*! No, of course I haven't. I haven't said anything. Not one word. Why are you asking, Tom?"

"Because I'm scared, Huck. I'm scared of Injun Joe."

"I know. Injun Joe will kill us if he finds out. If we say anything, we'll die. I'll never tell anyone, Tom. Don't worry. Come on, let's make our promise again. Then we'll both feel better."

And the boys made their promise again.

"I'm sorry about Muff Potter," said Tom. "All the townspeople are talking about him. They hate him. They say he's a murderer. But he isn't and he isn't a bad man."

"Yes, I know. I feel bad, too. He's done a lot for us. He's shown me some of the best places to fish. He's given me apples sometimes. I like him, but what can we do, Tom? We can't help him to escape. The people in the town will kill him if they find him. What can we do?"

"I don't know. But, let's go to the jail. Let's take him some food or something. *We'll* feel better and *he'll* feel better."

Tom and Huck went to the jail. Muff looked miserable and scared. When he saw the boys, he smiled. "Thank you, boys. You've been very kind to me. Kinder than anyone. I've helped a lot of the people in the town, but no-one comes to see me. You're really good boys. Thank you."

Tom went home, miserable. He felt really bad about Muff Potter. That night, he had horrible dreams.

Stop & Check

1 Match the questions and answers.

1 [e] What trick did the boys play?
2 ☐ Why was Tom bored?
3 ☐ Why did Huck pray?
4 ☐ How long was Tom sick?
5 ☐ Why did Tom feel worried and scared?
6 ☐ Who were the townspeople talking about?
7 ☐ Why did Tom and Huck go to the jail?
8 ☐ How did Muff Potter feel about the boys?

a For three weeks.
b Muff Potter.
c Because he didn't want Tom to die.
d They felt bad about Muff Potter.
e They caught Mr. Dobbins' hat and pulled it off.
f That they were good and kind.
g Because he was thinking about Injun Joe.
h Because the summer vacation was long.

Vocabulary

2 Find the words about school in the word-snake. Then put them into the right column.

bellteachergeographystudentgymdeskhistorypapermathpresidentchalkjanitorsciencecalculator

people	subjects	things
teacher		

Speaking for Key

3a Here is some information about a school play. Use the words to write questions about the information.

Town School	*End of School Show*
Poems & Stories from all the students	

July 1 / Light refreshments available
Starts 7.30 pm
For more information: ask Mr. Dobbins

1 where?   *Where is the show?*
2 what/hear?   _____
3 food?   _____
4 🕐 ?   _____
5 date?   _____
6 more info?   _____

3b Work in pairs. Ask and answer your questions.

Before-reading Activity

Listening

▶ 8 **4a** Listen to the first part of Chapter Six. Are these statements true (T) or false (F)? Tick the correct box.

		T	F
1	Tom goes to find Huck.	☑	☐
2	The boys are scared of Injun Joe.	☐	☐
3	The boys wait inside the courtroom.	☐	☐
4	Everyone believes Injun Joe.	☐	☐
5	Tom goes to see Muff's lawyer.	☐	☐
6	He doesn't tell the lawyer everything.	☐	☐
7	The lawyer calls Tom into the courtroom.	☐	☐

4b Now read Chapter Six and check your answers.

Chapter Six

Saving Muff Potter

▶ 8 The next day, Tom went to find Huck. "Let's go to the courtroom. Maybe we'll hear some news."

"Yes, but I don't want to go inside," said Huck. "I'm scared of Injun Joe."

The boys waited outside the courtroom. People went in and came out.

"What's happening?" the boys asked.

The news was never very good. Muff's lawyer* wasn't doing a good job. He wasn't asking the right questions.

"I'm worried," said Tom. "I'm worried about Muff Potter."

"I'm worried too," said Huck.

The next day, the boys did the same thing; they waited outside the courtroom. Now, even some of the townspeople were talking about Muff's lawyer. Every time someone told their story, Muff's lawyer said, "I have no questions to ask."

Nobody thought the lawyer was doing a good job.

lawyer – a person who helps you if you have problems with the police

Injun Joe told his story. Everyone believed him. Again, Muff's lawyer said, "I have no questions to ask him."

Muff Potter was in trouble. He looked miserable. Tom knew what he had to do. That evening, he went to talk to Muff's lawyer. "I think I can help you. I think I can help Muff," said Tom.

He told the lawyer everything. All about the grave-yard and Injun Joe. All about the doctor. "But please don't say anything about Huck. I promised."

"You'll have to be strong," said the lawyer.

The next morning, Muff's lawyer stood up. He looked at the judge. He looked at all the people in the courtroom. He turned to the courtroom officer, "Call Thomas Sawyer," he said loudly.

Everyone looked very surprised. The courtroom officer went outside. He called Tom. Tom's face went white. He slowly went inside.

Tom stood in front of the judge. He stood in front of all the townspeople. He was very scared. Then, the lawyer spoke. "Thomas Sawyer, where were you hiding on the night of the murder?"

Tom was very scared. He tried to speak, but no words came out. He looked around the courtroom. He looked at Injun Joe. Then, very quietly, he said, "In the grave-yard."

"Speak a little louder," said the lawyer. "Don't be scared. You were …?"

"In the grave-yard."

All the people in the courtroom were whispering. "Tom Sawyer was there! He saw what happened!"

And Tom told the whole story. He told everyone about the shoe. But he didn't tell them about Huck. Then he told them about the knife. And he told them about Injun Joe.

Injun Joe looked at Tom. His face was hard and scary. Suddenly, Injun Joe jumped up. "I'm not listening to any more of this. I'll have you, Tom Sawyer! I'll have you!"

He pushed the people out of his way. He ran to the window. He broke the window and jumped out. Injun Joe escaped.

Tom was a hero again. His story was in the

newspaper. All his friends wanted to hear about it. They listened again and again.

All the townspeople were sorry about Muff Potter. They were all very kind to him. They said they were sorry. Muff was happy again. He wasn't a prisoner any more; he was free.

The sheriff and his men looked for Injun Joe. The sheriff offered money for information. No-one knew anything. No-one could find Injun Joe. Tom and Huck were still scared. They both had bad dreams. "I'll only be happy when Injun Joe is dead," thought Tom.

★★★

There are some things which a boy *has* to do in his life. One of these things is looking for treasure. This day now came to Tom. He went to find Huck. "It's time to find some treasure," said Tom.

"Where can we find the treasure, Tom?" said Huck. "Where do people *put* it?"

"You can find treasure *everywhere*. On islands. Buried under a dead tree. In an old box in a hole. Sometimes people bury it with a map. But most of the time it's in old houses. Houses with ghosts in them."

"And who does the treasure belong to?"

"Don't be stupid! It doesn't belong to our Sunday-school teacher, does it? It belongs to robbers, of course. Robbers hide it. They hide it and then they forget about it. Or they die. Then, one day, someone finds an old piece of paper. It's old and yellow. There's a secret message on the piece of paper. And there's a map on the piece of paper. You follow the map and you find the treasure."

"Where do you want to start then, Tom?"

"Well there are lots of dead trees around here. Why don't we start with a dead tree?"

"Yes!" said Huck. "Let's try the dead tree by Still House."

Tom and Huck went to Still House. They began to dig under the dead tree. "What are you going to do with your treasure, Huck?"

"I'm going to spend it. I'm going to spend it on good things to eat and drink. I'm going to go to every circus that comes to town. I'm going to have a wonderful time. What about you, Tom?"

"Well, I'm going to save some of my money. I'm going to buy a new knife. I'm going to buy a cow. And, I'm going to get married!"

"Get married?" said Huck. "That's stupid! You sound like an old man!"

The boys worked for about an hour. They didn't find anything. "There's nothing here," said Tom. "Perhaps we're looking in the wrong place."

Huck agreed. "Why don't we go to Cardiff Hill? There are lots of dead trees there."

They went over to Cardiff Hill. They tried there, but they didn't find anything. The boys went from dead tree to dead tree. After all their digging, they were very tired.

"Let's stop for the day. We can try the old house tomorrow. The one with the ghost," said Tom.

The next day, the boys went to the old ghost house. The windows were all broken. It was old and dirty. It smelled old, too. Tom and Huck quietly went inside. They opened an old cupboard, but there was nothing inside. They looked in the rooms downstairs. They looked under the floor. Then they went upstairs. "Shh!" said Tom.

"What is it?" whispered Huck.

"Shh! It's voices. Can you hear them? Someone's outside!"

The boys were very quiet. They looked through a broken window. They could see two men. One of the men looked hard and angry. The other man was digging. Then the man who was digging said, "Hey! There's something here! I can feel it. It's an old box!"

Both Tom and Huck knew the man's voice. It was Injun Joe!

After-reading Activities

Stop & Check

1 Choose the best answer - A, B or C.

1 Why does Tom speak to the lawyer?
  A He wants to help Muff Potter
  B He's afraid of Muff Potter
  C The townspeople know about the murder

2 What does Injun Joe say to Tom Sawyer?
  A "I don't like you."
  B "I'll have you."
  C "Help me, Tom!"

3 Where do Tom and Huck first look for treasure?
  A Under a dead tree
  B On an island
  C Near the school

4 What does Huck want to do with his money?
  A Eat lots of good food and go to circuses
  B Buy a house in town
  C Build a house on Jackson's Island

5 What does Tom want to do with his money?
  A Leave school
  B Go on a long vacation
  C Buy a knife, buy a cow and get married

6 Who do the boys see in the old house?
  A Becky Thatcher
  B Huck's father
  C Injun Joe

Grammar

2 **Prepositions Treasure Hunt. Where's the key to the treasure? Follow the instructions below and find out.**

start here
↓

⑨	4	A	6	D	5	C	V	3	B
F	J	7	2	3	9	1	2	X	C
R	U	A	8	5	Y	G	3	S	P
W	L	7	T	6	D	H	2	N	K
V	8	4	2	P	L	J	7	6	G

Go right until you find a number 6. Go down 3 spaces, then go left 2 spaces. Go up until you find a number 4. Go right to the end of the line. Go down to the K, then go left to the letter between 6 and H. Go down 1 space. The key is in the space on your right .... You're rich!

Before-reading Activity

Speaking

3a **In Chapter Seven, Becky invites everyone to a picnic in the forest. Work in pairs. Imagine you are planning a picnic. Make notes about**

- where you are going
- when you are going
- what you are going to eat
- what you are going to drink
- what activities you are going to do

3b **Exchange ideas with another group.**

Chapter Seven
Becky's Picnic

▶ 10   Tom and Huck were really scared. Injun Joe was right outside. The boys watched and listened. The two men pulled the box out of the hole. Injun Joe opened the box. "It's gold! There's gold in here! Lots and lots of gold!" he said.

The two men came inside with the box. Now the boys were prisoners! There was no way out. Tom and Huck looked through a hole in the floor. They could see the two men. The men were looking at the gold. Then Injun Joe said, "We need to bury it. Let's go back to Number Two. I don't think Number One is safe, now."

The other man agreed. Then they both left the old house.

The two boys waited until it was safe. Then they left the house, too. "All that gold!" said Huck. "It was nearly ours. Now Injun Joe's got it."

"Yes, I know. I've never seen so much money. But where is he going to bury it? And where is

'Number Two'? We need to find out, Huck. We need to find out."

That night, Tom dreamt about gold. He dreamt about digging for treasure. But in the morning, he wasn't sure. "Did I dream about Injun Joe and the gold? Or was it real?" he asked himself. "I need to find Huck. Huck can tell me."

Huck was by the river. He was fishing. "No, it wasn't a dream. It was real," said Huck. "All that gold was real."

"But where are they staying?" said Tom. "We need to find out. Then we can follow them. We can find the treasure. I think Injun Joe's friend looks like that Spanish man. He's staying in a house near Cardiff Hill. Perhaps he's staying in a house with a number two?"

The boys went up to Cardiff Hill. They secretly went to the place where the Spanish man was staying. On the door, there was a number two. They made a plan. They decided to watch the house.

★★★

Becky Thatcher was back from her summer

vacation. Tom was very pleased. He forgot about Injun Joe and the treasure. At the moment, Becky was more important.

Becky and Tom spent most of the day together. "Tonight, I'm going to ask my mother about my picnic," said Becky. "She talked about it weeks ago. I hope she remembers. I hope she'll say yes."

"That's a great idea!" said Tom. "I hope she says yes, too!"

Becky asked and asked. In the end, Mrs. Thatcher agreed. "Yes, but stay with Susan Harper. It's a long way home from the river. And the picnic will finish late tomorrow. You mustn't walk home in the dark."

Becky told all her friends. "We can take the ferry-boat to the forest. We can make a camp. Then we can play in McDougal's cave*!" said Becky.

McDougal's cave was a favorite place. It was big and dark. There were lots of corridors. Everyone in the town knew *some* of the cave. But no-one alive knew *all* of the cave.

cave – a place (often inside a mountain) like a big hole that you can go into or live in

The next day, the ferry-boat took everyone down the river. In the forest, everyone climbed trees and laughed and played. When they were all hot and tired, they all went back to the camp. They ate and ate, until they were full of good food. After lunch, they rested under the trees and chatted. Then someone said, "Come on. Get the candles*. Who's ready for the caves?"

They all went up to McDougal's cave. They went in pairs and groups. Tom and Becky went together. Everyone went down different dark corridors. They jumped out at each other. They tried to surprise each other. They tried to scare each other. It was great fun. Then, one by one, everyone went back to the entrance. Hot and dirty, but smiling and happy. It was beginning to get dark. They all went back to the ferry-boat. Nobody saw, but two people were missing. Tom and Becky. Tom and Becky were lost in the cave.

★★★

That night, Huck watched Number Two. Injun Joe and the Spanish man came out. Huck followed

candle –

them; he followed them to the river. He followed them to Mrs. Douglas' house. There was a light in the window. There were people inside the house.

"I'm going to hurt Mrs. Douglas," said Injun Joe. "I'm going to cut off her ear!"

"Why, Joe? What did she do?" said the Spanish man.

"*She* didn't do anything, but her husband did. Her husband was a judge. He's dead now, but I don't care. He sent me to jail. I hated him. I want to hurt her. Let's wait for her visitors to go. Then I'll try."

Huck was very scared. He ran as fast as he could. He ran to Mr. Jones' house. "Mr. Jones! Mr. Jones! Don't say I told you. Don't say I told you. But it's Injun Joe. I heard him talking. He wants to hurt Mrs. Douglas. He wants to cut off her ear!"

Huck told Mr. Jones everything. Mr. Jones called his sons. They went to Mrs. Douglas' house. They waited behind some trees. Huck didn't want to go too near. He was scared. He waited and he listened. Then he heard the sound of a gun. He ran and ran, back to town.

The next morning, Huck went back to Mr. Jones' house. "Hello? Mr. Jones? Are you there? Are you all right?"

Mr. Jones opened the door. "Welcome Huck! Welcome. Yes, we're all fine. We didn't get Injun Joe. I'm sorry about that. But Mrs. Douglas is safe. That's thanks to you, Huck. The sheriff and his men are looking for Injun Joe. I hope they find him. Now, come and have some breakfast. You're a hero, Huck. I want everyone to know."

"NO! Please don't tell anyone. Injun Joe will kill me. PLEASE, Mr. Jones."

"All right, Huck. I'll keep quiet."

★★★

There wasn't any Sunday-school during the vacation. But everyone was in church early. Everyone was talking about Injun Joe and Mrs. Douglas. Mr. Jones was a hero. His sons were heroes, too. Mrs. Harper came into church. Susan was with her. Mrs. Thatcher went to talk to her. "Is Becky still asleep at your house?" she asked.

"Your Becky? I don't understand. She didn't stay with me last night," said Mrs. Harper.

Mrs. Thatcher's face went white. Then, Aunt Polly came into church. "Has anyone seen my Tom? He didn't come home last night. Did he stay with any of you last night?"

One by one, everyone said no. Then, Ben Rogers quietly said, "Perhaps they're still in the cave!"

Mrs. Thatcher and Aunt Polly started crying. All the women in the church came to look after them. All the men went to the ferry-boat. They went to McDougal's cave.

The men searched all day and late into the night. They couldn't find Tom and Becky. They searched the next day. Then, the next day and the next. In the end, everyone decided Tom and Becky were dead.

Stop & Check

**1 Fill the gaps in the summary of Chapter Seven. Use one
word from the box for each gap.**

> gold • picnic • cave • watch
> scared • dead • took • home

Tom and Huck saw Injun Joe and the Spanish man find
some (**1**) _gold_ in the old house. They were scared, so
they hid in the house. Injun Joe and the Spanish man
(**2**) _____ the gold away. Tom and Huck decided to
(**3**) _____ the Spanish man's house. When the day of
Becky's (**4**) _____ arrived, everyone was very happy.
They played in the forest, ate some very good food and
then they went into McDougal's (**5**) _____. When it was
dark, everyone went (**6**) _____, except for Tom and
Becky; they were lost in the cave. Huck heard that Injun
Joe wanted to hurt Mrs. Douglas. He was (**7**) _____, so
he asked Mr. Jones for help. People from the village were
scared, too; they thought Tom and Becky were (**8**) _____.

Writing

**2 Your friend, Huck, is very sick. You can't visit him. Complete
the message for him.**

Dear Huck,

I'm sorry _____ I hope you

_____

When you get well, let's _____

_____

xox

_____

Speaking for Key

3 Work in pairs. Ask and answer the questions and follow-ups about your daily life.

1 Do you live in the town or the country?
Tell me about your house.
2 What subjects do you study at school?
Tell me about your favourite teacher.
3 How much homework do you do?
Tell me about your favourite subject.
4 What do you like to read?
Tell me about your favourite book.
5 What type of TV programmes do you like?
Tell me about your favourite programme.

Before-reading Activity

Listening

▶ 11 **4 Listen to beginning of Chapter Eight. Choose A, B or C. Listen twice.**

1 Who is lost in the cave?
A Tom & Becky   **B** Amy & Alfred   **C** Mr. Dobbins

2 What does Tom use to find his way back to Becky?
A the chalk   **B** a candle   **C** his memory

3 Why does Becky cry?
A she's angry   **B** she's tired   **C** she's lazy

4 Who does Tom see in the cave?
A the Spanish man   **B** Injun Joe   **C** Aunt Polly

Chapter Eight

McDougal's Cave

▶ 11 In the cave, Tom and Becky didn't know what to do. They were lost. They were prisoners in there; they didn't know how to get out. They were cold and tired and they needed to sleep. When they woke up, Tom looked and looked for a way out. He was very clever, he used his piece of teacher's chalk. He used it to find his way back to Becky. But, Tom couldn't find a way out of the cave.

"Is it day or night?" said Becky. "How long have we been here? It feels like days."

"I don't know," said Tom. "I think we've been here for a long time, our candle's nearly finished."

Becky began to cry. "Oh, Tom! I'm tired and hungry; I don't want to die in here!"

"Don't worry, Becky. I'll find a way out."

Tom went down one corridor, and then another. Suddenly, he heard a noise. Was someone there? He went towards the noise and he saw a light from a candle. Then, at the end of the corridor, in the light of the candle, he saw Injun Joe. Injun Joe was here, in the cave, looking at his gold.

★★★

12 "They're here! We've found them, they're safe! They're here!" shouted Mr. Jones. "Find Judge Thatcher and the others! Tell them Tom and Becky are here! Everyone can stop looking for them now."

Lights went on all over town. People came out of their houses in their nightclothes. Tom and Becky were coming down the street with some workmen.

Home at last, Tom lay on the sofa. Everyone wanted to listen to his story and he was delighted to tell it. "We tried and tried to find a way out, but it was impossible. We were very hungry and very tired. Finally, I saw a small light. There was a hole. It was a way out! We were really happy. It was difficult to get through the hole, but we did it. Then, we saw some workmen. We told them our story and asked for their help. They gave us some food and they told us to rest. Then, they brought us here."

After their adventure in the cave, Tom and Becky were sick in bed. Tom was sick for three days.

Becky was in bed for a week.

When Tom felt a little better, he went to see Huck. Huck told Tom all about Mrs. Douglas, Injun Joe and the Spanish man. "The Spanish man is dead. They found his body in the river. He was trying to hide or to escape from the sheriff," said Huck.

Huck was pleased to hear all about Tom's adventures, too. Tom told him all about Injun Joe and the treasure. "The gold's in the cave, Huck. I know where it is! When I'm feeling stronger, we can go and get it."

A few days later, Tom went to see Becky. He met Judge Thatcher outside the house. "Hello, Tom," said the judge. "Thank you again for saving Becky. You're a good and honest boy and you were very clever to find a way out of the cave. But now the cave is safe. There won't be any more cave adventures for you, or for *anyone*."

"Why?" said Tom.

"Well, the day after you two came home, I closed the cave with a big, heavy, metal door. So, I'm happy to say, *no-one* can get in or out of there now."

Tom's face went white. "But, Judge Thatcher, Injun Joe was in the cave! I saw him there."

The judge's face went white, too. He quickly called some of the other men. They ran off to the cave. They pulled and pulled at the heavy metal door. Finally, they opened the cave. There was Injun Joe. He was dead.

★★★

After Injun Joe's death, Mr. Jones spoke to Mrs. Douglas. "It was Huck who saved you, not me. He was scared of Injun Joe, so I promised not to tell anyone. Now you need to know."

"He's a hero," said Mrs. Douglas. "But poor Huck. He has a hard life. He needs love and he needs a good home. Perhaps he'd like to come and live with me."

Mrs. Douglas told everyone that Huck was a hero. Huck went to live with her, but he didn't like it much. He had to wear nice clothes and he had to go to church. He liked his old clothes and he liked to be free. After three days, he ran away. Tom went to find him. "If you stay with Mrs. Douglas, you can be in my gang," said Tom. "Go on. Stay with her."

In the end, Huck agreed. "It'll be good to be part of a gang, especially your gang, Tom."

Together, the boys made a plan to get the gold. "I made some lines with chalk in the cave," said Tom. "We'll follow them from the hole. The hole that Becky and I found. The chalk will show us where the gold is. It'll show us how to get out, too."

The next day, the two boys climbed through the hole. They found Tom's line of chalk. They carefully followed it down one of the dark corridors, then they turned down another corridor. More chalk. Another corridor, and another one. At last, there, at the end of one of the corridors, they found a large box. "This is it!" said Tom. This is the gold!"

They slowly opened the box. Treasure! The box was full. It was full of gold! They were rich.

★★★

Now Tom was rich. He loved Becky and Becky loved him. And they loved each other even more after their time in the cave.

But, dear reader, here I must end my story. I am sorry, but my story is the story of a boy. It is the story of Tom Sawyer. If I do not end Tom's story here, it will become the story of a man.

Stop & Check

1 **Are these statements true (T) or false (F)? Correct the false statements.**

		T	F
1	Tom finds a way out of the cave.	☑	☐
2	Tom and Becky are sick after their adventure.	☐	☐
3	Mrs. Douglas is looking after Huck.	☐	☐
4	The Spanish man is alive.	☐	☐
5	Judge Thatcher is very angry with Tom.	☐	☐
6	Injun Joe is dead in the cave.	☐	☐
7	Tom and Huck find the treasure: they're rich.	☐	☐

Glossary Work

2a **Glossary Anagrams. Can you work out the anagrams? Use the clues to help you. All the words are in the glossary.**

1 bcektu   _bucket_   You can put paint or water in this.
2 aegnrrst s_____ Someone you don't know.
3 ceefn   f_____ Tom paints this in Chapter One.
4 ehiprsw w_____ When you talk very quietly, you .....
5 acdeln   c_____ Tom and Becky need this in the cave.
6 aelrwy   l_____ Someone who helps you if you have problems with the police.
7 abld   b_____ If you don't have any hair, you are .....

2b **Choose two words from the glossary. Make two anagrams. Can your partner work them out? Don't forget to put the first letter for each word. And don't forget a definition.**

Speaking

3 **Reading Quiz. Work in pairs to answer the quiz.**

ARE YOU A BOOKWORM?

1 How many books do you read a year?

a ☐ none
b ☐ two or three
c ☐ ten or twenty
d ☐ _____

2 Where do you get your books from?

a ☐ bookshops
b ☐ online
c ☐ as presents
d ☐ _____

3 Tick the sort of books you like best.

a ☐ thrillers
b ☐ adventure
c ☐ love stories
d ☐ historical drama
e ☐ biographies
f ☐ other non-fiction
g ☐ science fiction
h ☐ _____

4 What's your favorite book? _____
_____
_____

Writing

4 **Did you enjoy *The Adventures of Tom Sawyer*? Write your opinion.**

I liked/didn't like *The Adventures of Tom Sawyer*, because
_____
_____

My favorite character was _____, because
_____

My least favorite character was _____, because
_____

87

Mark Twain (1835 – 1910)

Mark Twain is sometimes called the father of the American novel. He was also a journalist and a public speaker, as well as an inventor. He made a lot of money from his writing, but lost a lot of it in business.

Mark Twain

Early Life

Mark Twain's real name was Samuel Langhorne Clemens. He was born in Missouri, USA, in a small town called Florida. He was born on November 30, 1835. At this time, people could see Halley's Comet in the sky: you can see this comet from Earth every 75 or 76 years. When he was very young, the family moved to a small town in Missouri called Hannibal. Twain's father was a lawyer and his mother was famous for her sense of humor and her beauty. They had seven children, but four of them died young. Then, when Twain was eleven years old, his father died.

Early Working Life

After the death of his father, Twain got a job with a printer. At first, he worked in Hannibal, but then he moved to New York. For the next few years, he worked in several different US cities. One day, Twain was traveling to New Orleans down the Mississippi.

On the journey, he decided he wanted to be a pilot on a steamboat (see picture). He had to study very hard to get his pilot's license: a pilot had to understand the river and the Mississippi is more than 3,200 km long. Twain worked as a pilot for a few years, until the start of the American Civil War, in 1861.

Giant Steamboats at New Orleans, 1853

Writing Career

Mark Twain wrote a lot of articles for newspapers, especially humorous articles. He also wrote travel books. His two most famous novels are *The Adventures of Tom Sawyer* and *Adventures of Huckleberry Finn*. Later in his life, he wrote two historical novels; *The Prince and the Pauper* and *A Connecticut Yankee at the Court of King Arthur*. They were about politics and society. Mark Twain also wrote about other writers' work. Sometimes, he was very rude about the other writers. As well as writing, Twain also worked as a public speaker. He was very famous for his sense of humor.

Illustration from the first edition of *The Adventures of Tom Sawyer* (1876)

Family Life

In 1870, Mark Twain married Olivia Langdon. They had four children; three daughters and a son. Their son died when he was a baby. The family lived in Connecticut and spent time in New York. They spent almost twenty years in Connecticut and today there is a museum in the house where they lived. Mark Twain's later family life was unhappy: two of his daughters and his wife died before him. In 1909, Twain talked about Halley's Comet and his death, "I came in with Halley's Comet in 1835. It is coming again next year, and I expect to go out with it".

He was right, he died on April 21, 1910, when Halley's Comet was very close to the Earth.

Olivia Langdon, Mark Twain's wife

Task

Complete the form with the information about Mark Twain.

Real Name: _____

Place of Birth: _____

Date of Birth: _____

First Job: _____

Some Famous Books: _____

Wife's Name: _____

Number of Children: _____

Date of Death: _____

The Mississippi River

The Mississippi is the fourth longest river in the world, after the Nile, the Amazon and the Yangtze.

Physical Geography

The **source** of the Mississippi River is Lake Itasca in northern Minnesota and its **mouth** is in the Gulf of Mexico. In total, the river is 3,734 km long. It is divided into three: the Upper Mississippi, the Middle Mississippi and the Lower Mississippi. At its widest point, Lake Winnibigoshish, the river is nearly 18 km wide. The Upper Mississippi has 43 **dams** (see pictures) to control the water. There are many natural and man-made lakes along the river, but there is only one waterfall; Saint Anthony's Falls. The Upper and Lower Mississippi have some important **tributaries**. They include the Missouri, the Illinois and the Red River. The Mississippi River **watershed** is the fourth largest in the world; it includes 31 US states and two provinces of Canada.

Dam on Upper Mississippi River, Minnesota

Saint Anthony falls, Minneapolis

Aerial view of Alton (Illinois) and The Clark bridge

Mississippi River Bridge

Flooding on the Mississippi

People and the Mississippi

Native Americans first built villages near to the Mississippi, because the land was very good for farming. The name 'Mississippi' comes from a Native American language. Later, Spanish and French explorers made maps of the river. French culture and language are still important in many areas along the river.

Of course, the Mississippi was very important for navigation. Between the 1820s and the 1870s, steamboats carried people, and **goods** like cotton and food, along the river. Some steamboats were like hotels on the river: they traveled between St. Louis and New Orleans. Mark Twain wrote a book about river transport called *The Life of the Mississippi*.

The first bridge across the Mississippi opened in 1855 and the first railroad bridge came a year later.

Task

Internet Research.

Choose an important river from your country. Find out about its physical geography and how people use it. Write a paragraph about it.

The Environment

Flooding is a big problem for the people who live along the Mississippi River. This happens because of **hurricanes**, rain, snow or the level of the sea. To stop their cities, towns and villages from flooding, governments build dams and **canals** to control the water. They also build **levees** to hold the water in the river. Sometimes, this is not enough. There have still been many serious floods along the Mississippi: many people have died and many more have lost their homes and businesses. Engineers are working hard to find better ways of stopping flooding.

Glossary

source – the beginning of a river
mouth – the end of a river (usually at the sea)
dam – see pictures
tributary – a stream or river that goes into a larger one
watershed – the area of land that gives water to a river
goods – things that people buy or sell
flooding – when there is too much water in a river and the water goes onto the land
hurricane – a very large storm system
canal – a man-made river
levee – a hill of earth. It stops flooding

Schools in Tom Sawyer's Day

The Adventures of Tom Sawyer is set in the 1840s. Schools then were very different from today's schools. Let's find out how.

Students studying at a village school. Late 19th century.

Did everyone go to school?

No. In the US, Massachusetts was the first state to say that everyone had to go to school, but this wasn't until 1852. Many towns and villages had schools, but there was no real education system. This was the same in most countries in the world. There were always children, like Huckleberry Finn, who didn't go to school. There were a lot of private schools, so people with money could send their children there. At this time, there were a lot of people in most countries in the world who couldn't read or write.

What equipment did schools have?

Many schools had blackboards, after their invention in 1801. Schoolchildren didn't write on paper – pencils were very, very expensive. They had to write on slates (see picture) and they often had to write with a piece of rock. Not all children had chalk to write with and most schools had very few books.

A slate.

What subjects did students study?

At the time of Tom Sawyer, it was very important to teach students to read, write and do simple mathematics. Students learnt poetry by heart: by repeating and repeating poems until they remembered them. They learnt writing by copying from the blackboard. Of course, there were no calculators, so students learnt their math 'tables' ($2 \times 2 = 4, 3 \times 2 = 6, 4 \times 2 = 8$ etc.).

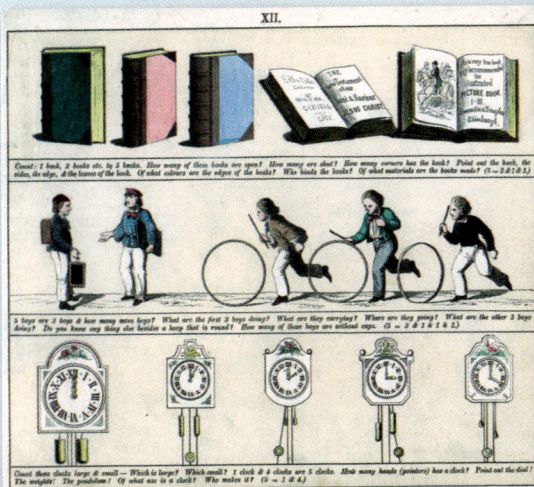

A page from a children's textbook. 1845.

What about punishment at school?

In *The Adventures of Tom Sawyer*, Tom is punished in different ways. Aunt Polly hits him with a stick and she also makes him do chores (work) at home. At school, teachers often hit children as a punishment. In many countries today, teachers can't hit students: they use non-physical punishments. In some states in America, including Mississippi and Louisiana, teachers can still hit students. Other punishments included standing in the corner and staying behind after school. Boys and girls were in the same class, but they didn't usually sit together: boys sat on one side of the class and girls sat on the other. A teacher sometimes made boys sit with the girls (or vice versa) as a punishment. Teachers also gave prizes for good behavior, often at the end of the school year.

Task

1 **Internet research. What did children do at recess in the nineteenth century? Find out about games they played, then try one of them with your friends.**

2 **Learn an English poem by heart!**

3 **Say your 9 times table. Example: one 9 is 9, two 9s are 18, three 9s are …**

TEST YOURSELF

How much can you remember about the story of *The Adventures of Tom Sawyer*? Use the clues to complete the crossword.

Clues Across

2 Tom has to paint the f_____ on Saturday. (5 letters)
3 Tom likes going s_____ . (8 letters)
6 Tom gets a bible as a p_____ . (5 letters)
9 Tom and Huck find the t_____ in the cave. (8 letters)
10 When Tom is ill, Huck says a p_____ . (6 letters)

Clues Down

1 Becky's father is a j_____ . (5 letters)
2 Tom and Huck often go f_____ . (7 letters)
4 Muff Potter isn't a m_____ . (8 letters)
5 Mr. Dobbins is a t_____ . (7 letters)
7 The boys make a c_____ on Jackson's Island. (4 letters)
8 Tom and Becky get lost in McDougal's c_____ . (4 letters)

Syllabus

Level A2

This reader contains the items listed below as well as those included in Level A1.

Nouns:

abstract nouns, compound nouns, noun phrases

Pronouns:

relative: *who, which, that*

Connectives

and, so, but, or, when, where, because, if

Adjectives:

opinion, description, classification, participles as adjectives, nationality, predicative and attributive

Prepositions:

places, time, movement, phrases, *like*

Verbs:

TENSE, ASPECT, FORM: Present Perfect Simple: indefinite past with *already* and *never*, unfinished past with *for* and *since*; Past Continuous: continuous action interrupted by the Past Simple, parallel past actions; Future with *going to; -ing* form after verbs and prepositions; Present Simple Passive; *will* for future reference, promises & predictions; *would ...like* for offers & requests; *need* for necessity & obligation; *could* for ability; *mustn't* for prohibition; *have to* for obligation; common phrasal verbs

Types of Clause

zero and type-one conditionals
defining relative clauses: *who, where,* zero pronoun
subordinate clause following *sure, know, think, hope, say, tell, if, where, when, because*

Teen (EH) Readers

Stage 1
Charles Dickens, *Oliver Twist*
Maureen Simpson, *In Search of a Missing Friend*
Mark Twain, *A Connecticut Yankee in King Arthur's Court*
Lucy Maud Montgomery, *Anne of Green Gables*

Stage 2
Maria Luisa Banfi, *A Faraway World*
Frances Hodgson Burnett, *The Secret Garden*
Mary Flagan, *The Egyptian Souvenir*
Robert Louis Stevenson, *Treasure Island*
Mark Twain, *The Adventures of Tom Sawyer*

Stage 3
Charles Dickens, *David Copperfield*
Anonymous, *Robin Hood*
Mary Flagan, *Val's Diary*
Maureen Simpson, *Destination Karminia*
Jack London, *The Call of the Wild*